easy
painted
HOME
DÉCOR

easy
painted
HOME
DÉCOR

GIGI WRIGHT

NORTH LIGHT BOOKS
CINCINNATI, OHIO
www.artistsnetwork.com

About the Author

Gigi Wright has a bachelor's degree in fine arts from Colorado Women's College and has been teaching her designs at seminars, conventions and studio classes for the past twenty years. She is an active member of the National Society of Decorative Painters and participates in local chapter activities. She is also a member of the Society of Craft Designers and is involved with the Knoxville Symphony League, helping with the art projects for their Show House and auctions. Gigi regularly has her art published in national craft magazines, is the co-author of *Etching to Paint* and author of *Tole Fairy Tales*, and has appeared in several DIY (Do-It-Yourself) Television segments, which are popular for home décor ideas.

Gigi resides in lush, green Knoxville, Tennessee, after spending most of her life growing up on the Arizona desert in Scottsdale. A joy in her life came last year in the form of a precious grandson, Logan.

You may visit Gigi's website at www.jeetles.com to see some of her other work, or you may e-mail her at fairysigns@aol.com.

08 07 06 05 04   5 4 3 2 1

Library of Congress Cataloging-in-Publication Division
Wright, Gigi
    Easy painted home décor / Gigi Wright
    p. cm.
    Includes index.
    ISBN 1-58180-536-5 (alk. paper)
    1. Painting--Technique. 2. Decoration and ornament
    3. House Furnishings. I. Title
    TT385.W75 2004
    745.7'23--dc22
                               2003071068

Editors: Liz Schneiders, Tonia Davenport
Designer and Photo Stylist: Mary Barnes Clark
Layout Artist: Kathy Gardner
Production Coordinator: Sara Dumford
Photographer: Christine Polomsky and Al Parrish

Metric Conversion Chart

to convert	to	multiply by
Inches	Centimeters	2.54
Centimeters	Inches	0.4
Feet	Centimeters	30.5
Centimeters	Feet	0.03
Yards	Meters	0.9
Meters	Yards	1.1
Sq. Inches	Sq. Centimeters	6.45
Sq. Centimeters	Sq. Inches	0.16
Sq. Feet	Sq. Meters	0.09
Sq. Meters	Sq. Feet	10.8
Sq. Yards	Sq. Meters	0.8
Sq. Meters	Sq. Yards	1.2
Pounds	Kilograms	0.45
Kilograms	Pounds	2.2
Ounces	Grams	28.3
Grams	Ounces	0.035

Dedication

My mother, Eugenia S. Paul, has always been a positive and driving force in my life, and I am dedicating this book to you, Mom. Thank you for all your encouragement and for all you do for me.

Also, I am dedicating this book to the memory of my sister, Anne, who dedicated her life's work to the history of art. She will always be remembered with love.

Acknowledgments

To all the special people in my life including my daughter Stacey, son Grant, friends Jeri, Judy, Ruth, Pinky, Lynn, Carol, Laura and Allen, Hugh, Linda and Allen, Ludie and J. Hugh, Carl and Eleonore, and John and Teri, I thank you for your encouragement, enthusiasm and support in my work.

Also, to my newly acquired friends at F&W Publications: Liz Schneiders, Christine Doyle and Christine Polomsky. I thank you for a tremendous and wonderful experience in working with such a professional team.

Thank you also to Loew-Cornell for the brushes, Delta Technical Coatings for the paint products, and Decorator & Craft Corp., Walnut Hollow and Viking Woodcrafts for all the wonderful surfaces used for demonstration purposes.

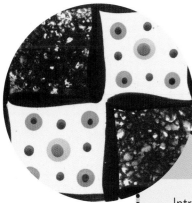

Contents

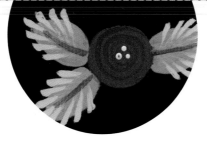

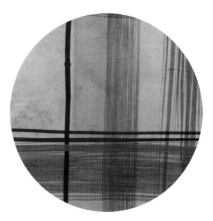

Contents

Projects continued

Introduction

There's so much pleasure to be had by decorating your home, giving it a lift or adding a few special pieces to make a room come together. The process is fun and creative, and you get to enjoy the results for years to come. We all love to surround ourselves with beautiful things and pretty colors because it makes us feel good. Creating those beautiful things ourselves makes us feel even better.

For years, I've taught people how to paint single pieces for their homes. In this book, I've taken the idea of decorating a step further by showing you how to paint ten simple motifs that you can adapt to any surface imaginable. I've included step-by-step instructions for painting each design, as well as techniques for painting on a wide variety of surfaces, so that you can paint one accent piece or create a united theme for an entire room.

The designs are varied to include ideas for the holidays, your patio or sunroom, kitchen, dining and family rooms, and kid's bedroom or bath. From simple checks and dots to bright flowers or elegant lemons, the designs can be adapted for any room in your house.

You don't need a fine arts degree to paint beautiful pieces that will be admired for years to come. Your interest and enthusiasm are all the background you need. Once you start painting these easy designs, your imagination will soar. Try substituting other colors for those that I've chosen, using ones that match your own décor. Get creative in your choice of surfaces. Look for pieces in any of your favorite local craft stores and discount department stores. They have surfaces at affordable prices that may need just a touch of paint to tie into your personal home décor.

Painting for your home is creative, fun and easy to do. It is my sincere wish for you to see that, by following my step-by-step instructions, you will create some beautiful results.

Materials

Before you get started with your painting, you will want to gather up a few supplies. Following are the materials used in this book. For information on locating a retailer for any of these materials, see the Resources on page 94.

Paints and Mediums

There are many wonderful paints and mediums on the market today that allow you to paint on virtually any surface. Below are the products I used in this book, along with an explanation of each so that you can use them in your own painting.

Acrylic paint: Bottled acrylics are water-based, nontoxic, fast-drying paints that come in a huge array of colors. I have used Delta Ceramcoat throughout this book.

Fabric medium: Mix this with your acrylic paints for fabric painting. It can also be used in the brush to blend paints for floated color on fabrics, and it helps to prevent fading when the fabric is washed.

acrylic paint

Candle and soap painting medium: Prepare a soap or candle surface with this medium before painting so that paint will evenly adhere to the surface without scratching off or beading up.

All-purpose sealer: Use a sealer to prepare wood or papier mâché surfaces so that the paint will spread evenly when applied. If the surface becomes slightly rough after the sealer is applied, simply sand lightly before painting.

Varnish: Use a water-based varnish to protect your painted designs, applying it after your painting has completely dried. Varnishes come in brush-on and spray forms and are available in gloss, matte and satin finishes. I prefer to use a brush-on satin for my projects.

Glass and ceramic paint: This is a specialty nontoxic paint formulated for use on nonporous surfaces such as glass, ceramics, metal and slate. There are a number of brands available. I use Delta Air-Dry PermEnamels. The PermEnamel system involves three easy steps: apply a surface conditioner, paint, then apply a glaze or protective coat. The products are intended to be used as a system with certain mediums and should not be mixed with any acrylic or other enamel paints.

Once your painted project has cured for ten days, the pieces are dishwasher safe, microwavable and ovenproof up to 350° F (177° C).

Surface conditioner: Wipe this alcohol-based conditioner on nonporous glass, tile and mirror surfaces before painting to enable PermEnamel paint to adhere to the surface. Allow it to dry a few seconds before painting. Be sure to use the surface conditioner formulated for the enamel paint you'll be using.

enamel paint

Metal surface conditioner: This is used to paint metal surfaces with PermEnamel paint. Other enamel paints systems may also require a conditioner specifically for metals.

Thinner: Use this product instead of water to thin Air-Dry PermEnamel paints if they become sticky or unmanageable, because water is not compatible with PermEnamels. Use only one drop to a paint puddle and mix to bring the paint back to a nice liquid state.

Glaze for enamel paints: This provides a protective coat for enamel paints. Instead of brushing it over the entire surface, I use it only on the painted part of the design. Again, use the glaze formulated for the enamel paint you are using. I use Clear Gloss Glaze for Air-Dry PermEnamels on high-gloss glass and ceramics and Satin Glaze for PermEnamels on etched glass or ceramics.

Brushes

The quality of a painter's brushes is directly reflected in the quality of the painted project. I recommend a good-quality brush, but I don't necessarily recommend that beginners buy the best and most expensive. First become familiar with how the brushes work; later you can invest in more expensive brushes.

In this book, I use the Loew-Cornell La Corneille Golden Taklon Series. These brushes are excellent synthetic bristle brushes that are readily available in most craft stores and craft sections of department stores. I like them because they are soft but have a lot of spring that allows them to retain their shape even after being bent.

Following are a few brushes I recommend you purchase as a basic set. Over time, as you do more painting, you can add brushes of different sizes and shapes to your collection.

Wash/glaze brush: This large flat brush is used for applying varnish or glaze mediums to finished pieces. It is also used to add a wash of color to large areas of a design.

Sponge brush: This very inexpensive brush is used to apply protective sealer to large wood, papier mâché, or metal surfaces. I don't recommended using it to apply varnish because it will create bubbles.

Flat brush: This brush is typically used when you're applying side-loaded or floated color (see page 17).

Angular brush: Also used for floating color, this brush's bristles are cut at an angle. It is wonderful to use for painting flower petals and roses.

Filbert brush: This brush's bristles are like those of the flat brush but the edges are cut to a more rounded shape. Use a filbert for strokes in flower petals and on bug wings and for basecoating small rounded areas of a design.

Round brush: Use this brush for basecoating small and rounded parts of a design and for pulling comma strokes (see page 20).

Round stroke brush: This brush is designed especially for strokework patterns and pulling comma strokes.

Deerfoot stippler brush: This is a round brush that has been cut at an angle to look like a little hoof. It is used to achieve a light, speckled look on a design and to create texture such as fur on a bear or sugar on candy and cookies.

Liner brush: Use this brush to create lines such as veins on leaves. It is an essential tool for painting. A medium-length bristle is best for beginner students.

Script liner brush: This brush has a longer bristles and is used for making longer lines without stopping to reload. It is a bit more difficult for a beginner student to use simply because of the length of the bristles.

Rake brush: This is a flat brush with a feathered end that is used for painting areas of a design with long, multilined strokes. Use it for painting plaids, grass, or hair and fur.

General Supplies

In addition to paints and brushes, there are a few other supplies that will help you in your painting. Here is a list of items I recommend having on hand.

Double-ended stylus: This tool is used for tracing patterns on surfaces without leaving a mark on the pattern, or for making small dots as part of a design.

stylus

Palette knife: Use this tool to blend paints with mediums and other colors on your palette.

Graphite paper: Also called transfer paper, it is used to transfer your pattern onto your painting surface. I have used black graphite to transfer patterns to light surfaces and white to transfer patterns to dark surfaces. White is easier to cover with paints, so use it whenever possible.

Sea sponge: Natural sponges (some with large holes and others with small holes) are used to create texture or "faux" texture and bring dimension to a design.

sea sponge

medium flat brush

rake brush

small flat brush

deerfoot stippler brush

round stroke brush

Basic Painting Techniques

Preparing a Wood Surface

From your favorite table and chairs to the chest of drawers passed down from generation to generation, painting on wood can be a fun and rewarding experience. But before you choose your motif and start painting, there are a few steps you must take to prepare the wood.

1. Apply Wood Filler

Dab on some wood filler to cover any rough spots and allow this to dry well.

2. Sand Surface

Sand the surface smooth with a medium-grit sanding block or sandpaper.

3. Seal Wood

Seal the wood with all-purpose sealer using a wide brush. Allow to dry completely.

4. Sand Surface Again

The sealer will raise the grain of the wood slightly. Lightly sand the surface again, using a fine-grit sanding block or sandpaper.

Preparing Other Surfaces

Other surfaces besides wood can also be decorated with beautiful motifs. Follow the instructions below for preparing papier mâché, metal, glass and fabric. If you follow a few simple rules for preparation, the sky is the limit as to what you can paint!

Preparing Papier Mâché

To prepare a papier mâché piece, apply all-purpose sealer to the surface and allow it to dry before basecoating.

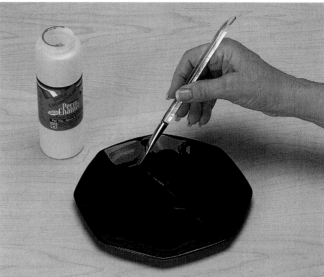

Preparing Glass Surfaces

Generously apply a surface conditioner over the entire surface to be painted. This will dry quickly and will leave the surface ready to accept enamel or glass paint.

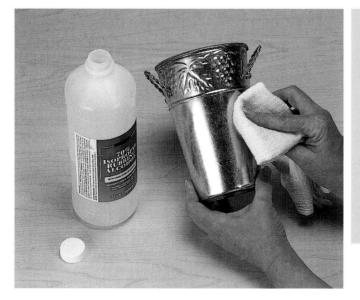

Preparing Metal Surfaces

Clean a metal surface with a soft cloth and rubbing alcohol before applying any conditioner or paint color.

Preparing Fabric Surfaces

Wash and iron fabric before painting to provide a smooth surface. To secure fabric while painting, lightly coat a large, flat piece of cardboard with spray adhesive and, with your hand, smooth the fabric down. This will provide a hard, secure surface to paint on.

Transferring a Pattern

The patterns for the motifs in this book appear on pages 88-93. Enlarge or reduce these on a photocopier to fit your surface. Below are two different ways to transfer the pattern to the surface.

Transferring a Random Pattern

For smaller surfaces or for designs with a looser placement of elements, trace the pattern on pieces of tracing paper. Arrange the elements as you transfer them to the surface with graphite paper and a stylus. To vary the design, turn some of the pieces of tracing paper over and transfer the elements so that they face the opposite direction.

Transferring a Repeating Pattern

For large surfaces or designs that repeat, but are connected, trace the shape of the surface onto tracing paper, then arrange the elements of the design on the surface pattern. Once you have the design arranged to your satisfaction, transfer all the elements to the surface by placing graphite paper between the tracing paper and the surface. Trace over the design with a stylus.

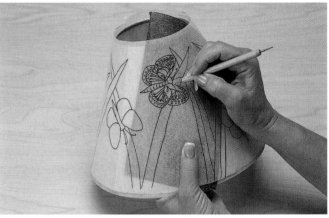

Preparing a Palette

Whether I am in a dry or humid climate, I always use a wet palette so that my paints stay soft during the time I am painting. To prepare your palette, you will need a low-lipped tray, one paper towel and a piece of deli wrap paper.

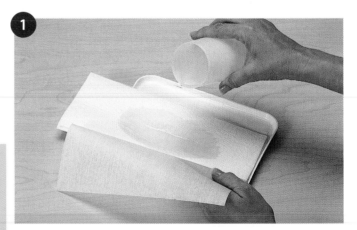

1. Secure Paper

Place the folded paper towel inside the folded deli paper. Pour a small amount of water on top of the paper towel, enough so the towel is damp. Lay the top of the deli paper over the wet towel. Smooth it out to remove any excess water.

2. Add Paint

Place your paint on top of this palette. The paints should remain usable for several hours.

Basecoating Basics

A carefully applied basecoat will help to give your painted piece a professional look. Whether you basecoat with a brush or a roller, take time to apply a smooth coat of paint and let the paint dry thoroughly between coats.

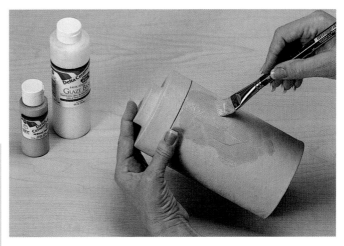

Basecoating with a Brush

Use a ¾-inch (19mm) or 1-inch (25mm) wash brush to basecoat your surface with two coats of paint, allowing it to dry between coats.

Basecoating with a Roller

For basecoating a large, flat surface such as a place mat, centerpiece or floorcloth, use a 3-inch (76mm) foam craft roller. The paint will go on quickly and evenly. Wash out the foam roller and allow the painted surface to dry before applying a second coat. If you are texturing the background with another color, it may not be necessary to apply a second coat.

Helpful Hint

By using a water-dampened brush for basecoating, your paint will slide on more easily without leaving brush lines. It is necessary to wait for it to dry before applying another coat, but when it does dry, there will be no lines as the slightly thinned paint will settle better.

Sealing with Varnish

Once you have put your time and energy into a project, you will want to be sure to protect it from the elements. This is especially important for frequently used pieces or those placed in high-traffic areas.

On some projects, I have applied seven or eight coats of varnish, sanding with a piece of very fine steel wool after every two coats have dried overnight. Then, after the eighth coat has dried, I buff it with beeswax to create a wonderful luster finish. I do this for very fine pieces of furniture or intricate décor items. This is a time-consuming process that you won't want to do for every project. Even a few coats of varnish will do the trick to ensure that your piece stays beautiful a long time.

Protect the Surface

Brush on several coats of varnish with a large wet brush to protect the surface. Allow the surface to dry between coats. If you start with a wet brush, the varnish will go on more evenly.

Loading the Brush

Learning to load and use your brushes properly will make your paintings look better, and it will make the painting process much more enjoyable for you. The techniques below will help you to load a brush for basecoating, whether you're painting the entire surface or a small area of the design, and for painting a wash. A wash is paint thinned with water to make it light and in some cases transparent. Applying a wash to your painting allows you to add a little color at a time to get just the right amount.

Loading for Basecoating

To load a flat brush for painting areas of solid color, place the brush with all bristles flat (not on a corner of the brush) into the side of the paint puddle. You will have much more control of the amount of the paint you are loading if you pull the paint from the side. Try to avoid having the paint completely cover the brush. For tips on basecoating a surface, see page 15.

Loading for Painting a Wash

To make a watered-down paint pigment, called a wash, apply extra water to the brush and pull a very small amount of paint from the side of the puddle. A heavy wash, also called a sheer base, contains considerably more pigment than a light wash.

Side Loading a Brush

The side loading technique is generally used with a flat, angular or filbert brush. This method of loading the brush produces a stroke that has strong color on one side but fades off to a soft edge on the other side.

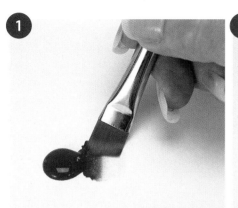

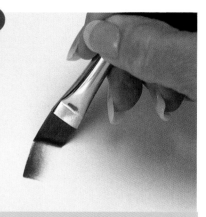

1. Place Brush in Paint

Place the corner of the brush into the side of the paint puddle.

2. Add Paint

Work the paint into the bristles by passing the brush back and forth next to the puddle. Stay on the same blending track and work the paint through, not off, the brush. The idea is to have paint on one side of your brush that fades to no paint (clear) on the other.

3. Float Color

When you have blended the paint through the brush but not all the way to the other side, you are ready to make the stroke. This is called floated color. It is useful in shading and highlighting techniques to give objects more dimension.

Double Loading a Brush

Loading one color onto each side of your brush is called double loading. You can achieve beautiful, blended effects with this technique.

1. Load Brush

Load your brush (in this case, a filbert) with the first color by flipping the brush back and forth in the paint from the side of the puddle until all bristles are covered.

2. Add Second Color

Swipe the corner or one side of the brush into the second color from the side of the puddle.

3. Create Leaf Stroke

To create a leaf or petal, when using a double-loaded brush, press down flat with the bristles, then gently release, lift and turn the brush to the side to bring the stroke to a point.

Using a Liner Brush

Liner brushes are used to paint thin lines. They are also very useful for outlining and for making highlight strokes, borders and vein lines for leaves.

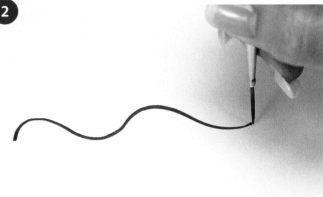

1. Load Brush

Load a wet liner brush with paint from the side of the puddle. Pull the brush out of the puddle and bring it to a point to ensure that there is an even amount of paint in the bristles and no glob at the end. Your paint should be the consistency of ink to make a good, clean line.

2. Pull Wavy Line

A liner brush can be used to pull a wavy line using steady hand pressure and holding the brush in a vertical position to create a long, thin, continuous line.

Using a Rake Brush

A rake brush is designed to get the look of multiple thin strokes all at once. The way to achieve this is to use the proper mix of paint and water. For long, thin, transparent lines, use more water in the brush and less paint. For lines that are wider and have a stronger color, use equal parts of pigment and water to make an ink-like consistency.

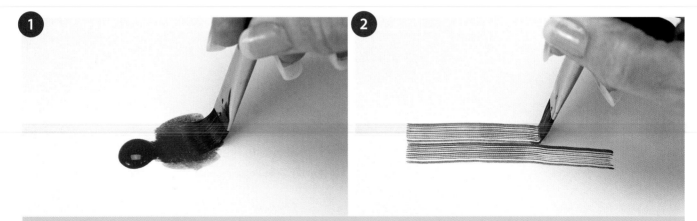

1. Load Brush

With a wet rake brush, pull some paint to the side of the puddle. Press the brush into the thinned paint to spread evenly into the bristles. The paint should look jagged on the bristles when held up. If the bristles are stuck together, there is a bit too much paint in the brush.

2. Pull Strokes

Pull a stroke placing the bristles very lightly on the surface. If you are making a double width, simply start next to the line you have finished. For an example of this technique, see the Plaid Floorcloth on page 36.

Making C-Strokes

There are a few basic brush strokes that will come in handy as you paint the motifs in this book. This stroke is slightly curved to look like the letter C. It is often used in decorative blended painting, and I use it frequently in this book to give a blended, dimensional look.

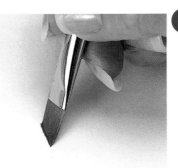

1. Hold Chisel Edge
Hold the brush on the chisel edge (on the tips of the bristles) to start the stroke.

2. Start the C
As you press down on the bristles, pull the brush to start the circle, making a C-curve.

3. Lift Chisel Edge
About half way around the stroke, start to gently lift up, and end on the chisel edge again.

Making "Chocolate Chip" Strokes

This little stroke, which consists of a quick flick of the wrist, resembles a chocolate chip.

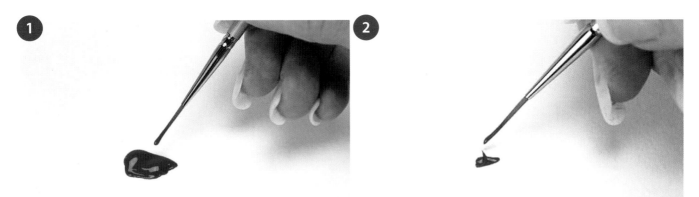

1. Load Brush
Load a no. 1 liner brush with paint, but do not try to make the paint even out in the brush. Leave a small glob at the end of the brush.

2. Lift and Flick Brush
Place the end of the brush horizontally on the surface as if you are setting it down. As you start to lift the brush, give it a slight flick to the side making a small point upward.

Making Commas and Teardrop Strokes

These strokes come in handy for highlights and borders. The more you practice making different kinds of strokes, the easier they will get.

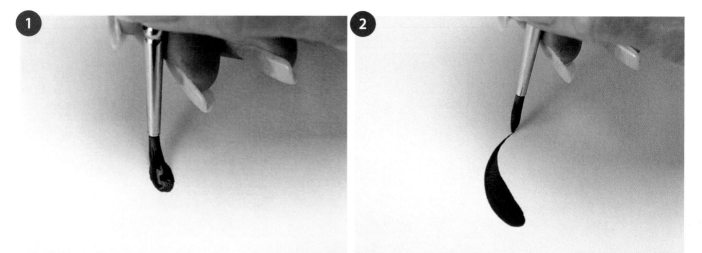

1. Press Brush Down

Start with a clean round brush. I use the round stroke brush because it makes very clean strokes. Fully load the brush and press down on your surface.

2. Pull Brush to a Point

As you lift to release the brush, pull it to a point. If you curve it to a point, it is called a comma stroke.

3. Pull Brush Straight

If you pull the stroke straight toward the center of your hand, the bristles will lift naturally. A straight stroke is a teardrop stroke. (See the Dots & Checks motif on page 24).

Stippling

Stippling is a paint effect that is typically done with a dry brush, simply because it is difficult to achieve a light and airy look when the brush is wet. This method is useful for making highlights and shadows, and for bringing softness to rounded objects.

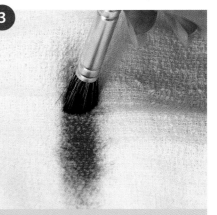

1. Load Paint Lightly
Place the long end of a deerfoot stippler or the center of a regular stippler very lightly into the side of the paint puddle, tapping off the paint to the side.

2. Tap Bristles
Continue to tap the bristles until you have only a small amount of paint left and there are no large globs appearing on the palette. To apply the paint to your project, tap the brush on the surface.

3. Clean Brush
To clean or change colors, dry-wipe the stippler on a soft cloth by rubbing briskly back and forth. You may not rid the brush of all paint, but it will be sufficient for changing colors. This is called using a "dirty brush". To get a cleaner brush, use hand sanitizer rather than water; the alcohol will make it dry faster.

Sponging

Similar to the effects of stippling, sponging is done with a damp sponge and usually produces a softer appearance than that of stippling.

1. Wet Sponge
Dip a damp or wet sponge into the paint puddle. The wetness of your sponge will determine the degree of color. The wetter the sponge, the lighter the color.

2. Tap Off Excess Paint
Tap the excess paint on the palette to check the amount you have in the sponge and to even out the pattern. Then tap the sponge onto your project. This technique is great for painting a textured or faux finish on a surface background.

Making Dots

Dots are a quick and easy way to fill the background of any beautiful motif.

1. Dip Stylus in Paint

Place the end of the stylus in the middle of a fresh paint puddle.

2. Lift and Dot

Lift the stylus from the paint and touch the end to your surface. Touching the surface again will produce a smaller dot. To create dots that are of equal-size, continue diping the end of the stylus in the paint puddle before painting each dot.

3. Make Larger Dots

Using the back end of a brush will make larger dots. As noted in step 2, dipping the end of the brush in paint before each dot is necessary to create dots of equal size.

Fixing Mistakes

We all make mistakes—it's human nature! But don't let a simple goof-up ruin your entire project. Follow the steps below, using a cotton swab. If your paint has cured (dried for several hours and become set), water or sanitizer will not remove it. Try using the background color to paint over the mistake.

Wipe with Hand Sanitizer

Use hand sanitizer on wet or freshly dry paint to thin the paint, and then wipe it off with a clean soft cloth. This works on porous and nonporous surfaces including wood, metal, glass, mirror and tile.

Wipe with Water

Wet a cotton swab and rub off excess paint. Then wipe the area with a clean rag. This works on all nonporous surfaces such as tile, glass, mirror and metal.

Add more surface conditioner before continuing your painted project.

Dividing a Circle

One last technique that will come in handy when you're painting for your home is an easy way to evenly space a design on a circle. When decorating a plate or another round object, it is important to space your design evenly for a balanced appearance. For this demonstration, I used a ½-inch (12mm) flat brush and a 10-inch (25.4cm) round dinner plate.

1. Paint Evenly Spaced Checks

Paint checks at four evenly spaced points on the plate.

2. Add More Checks

Paint more checks between the first four, spacing them evenly.

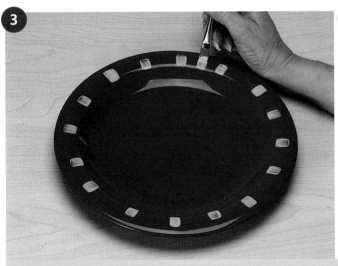

3. Fill in Between Checks

Fill in between the checks to keep them even.

4. Add Alternate Checks

Add a second row of alternate checks to complete the pattern.

Dots & Checks
tray

The idea of a sunroom

suggests light and cheerful tones to
me. What could be more cheerful than the
color yellow? This dot and check motif is easy, colorful and quick. Any or all of the simple palette colors can
be interchanged to create the look you prefer. For instance,
you could use light green for the squares or red for the
background. I like the fact that this project is fast and easy,
and that there are so many great surfaces you can use it
on. I've used a nice serving tray to show you how
it's done.

Materials

Wooden Tray
Square pop-up sponge
Varnish
Stylus
No. 1 Jackie Shaw liner brush
No. 12 flat brush
¾-inch (19mm) wash/glaze brush
Large-handled brush
Medium-handled brush
Small-handled brush

Delta Ceramcoat Paints

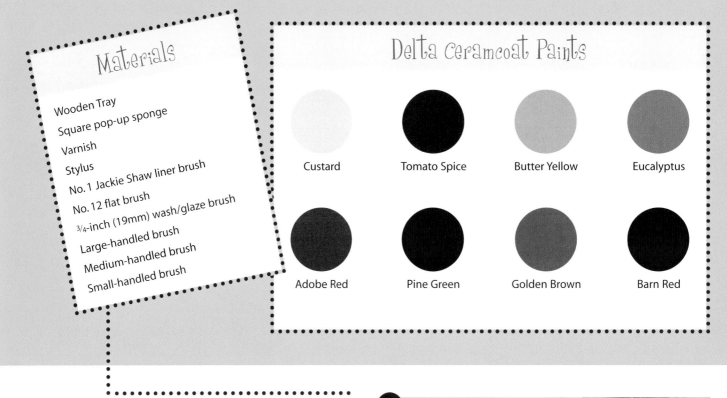

Custard

Tomato Spice

Butter Yellow

Eucalyptus

Adobe Red

Pine Green

Golden Brown

Barn Red

1. Basecoat Surface

Basecoat the surface using a ¾-inch (19mm) wash/glaze brush and Custard. Cut out a square pop-up sponge to an appropriate size for your border. Here, I am using a ¾-inch (19mm) square. Wet the sponge. Apply Tomato Spice paint to the sponge, using the no. 12 flat brush. Cover it well, but do not let it drip.

2. Create Checkerboard Pattern

Place the paint-covered sponge on the edge of the tray, starting in the center of one side. Create a checkerboard pattern, adding paint approximately every third application.

3. Add Yellow and Green Dots

Use a large brush handle to place a Butter Yellow dot in the center of each blank space. Then, using a medium brush handle, add four Eucalyptus dots around the center, yellow dot.

4. Add Red Dots

Using a small brush handle, add Adobe Red dots between the green dots. Set the tray aside for the dots to dry completely.

5. Add Green and Brown Dots

When the dots are completely dry (after one hour or so), use a double-ended stylus to paint smaller Pine Green dots on top of the lighter green dots. Next, paint smaller Golden Brown dots on top of the yellow dots.

6. Add Teardrop Strokes

With a no.1 Jackie Shaw liner brush and Barn Red, pull teardrop strokes (see page 20) along the edges of each sponged square to complete this motif. To protect your painted piece, brush with varnish, allowing the varnish to dry thoroughly between coats.

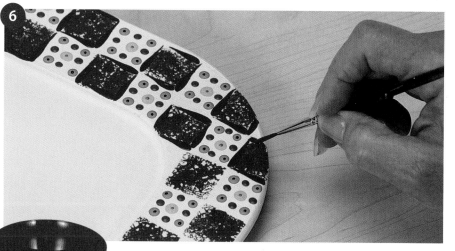

Mix Things Up!

Whew! If you didn't know how to sponge or dot before this project began, you sure do now! This technique will work on anything. Try it on glassware, coasters and fabric. Also try cutting the sponge in different shapes or sizes to go with the dots. This design does not have to be limited to borders. Try an overall motif or just the center of a surface. Vary the colors and be creative! Let your kids try it. This is a great technique for scout troops and children four years and older.

Sunroom Variation: Napkin

Painting on fabric is easy to do! Once you give it a try, you won't be able to stop coming up with great ways to incorporate it into your home décor.

This motif is so easy, you may find yourself adding dots and checks in many color combinations to everything from napkins to tote bags to aprons! A set of napkins, like the one here, is a great addition to the tray and goblets.

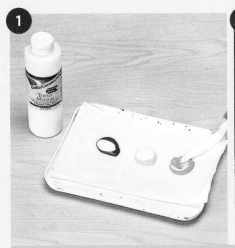

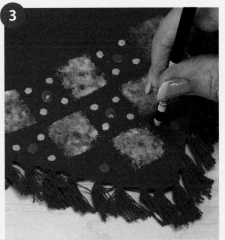

1. Mix Paint

For this method on fabric, use a palette knife to mix two parts of paint to one part fabric medium.

2. Create Checkerboard Pattern

Brush a mixture of Custard and fabric medium onto the sponge. Create a checkerboard pattern on the corner of a napkin.

3. Add Red and Green Dots

Add dots with the end of a paint brush dipped in Adobe Red and Eucalyptus. I stopped there, but you could further embellish with more colors from this palette.

Allow the paint to dry. To set the color, place it into a clothes dryer for about 20 minutes, or iron.

Roses & Checks
plate

Thinking about a new
set of dishes? Or do you want to give
the ones you've got a lift? Boy, is this design for
you! I like the sharp contrast of black plates with
bright colors, but this design works very well on other
colors, too! You can even use it on clear drinking glasses. If
you like to shake it up a little, experiment with a variety of
colors for the check part of the motif. The best part about
this design is its flexibility to accommodate numerous
surface sizes and shapes.

Materials

Plate
Surface conditioner
Thinner diluent
Stylus
Clear gloss glaze
No. 1 Jackie Shaw liner brush
No. 3 round brush
No. 12 flat brush

Delta PermEnamel Paints

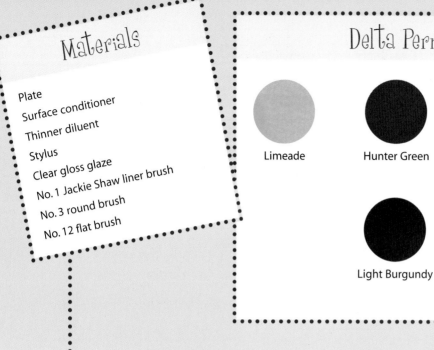

Limeade   Hunter Green   True Green   Red Red

Light Burgundy   Cotton Candy Pink

1. Apply Surface Conditioner

Generously apply the surface conditioner over the surface to be painted. This is step one of the PermEnamel system. It contains alcohol, so it dries quickly. Do not rub off.

2. Paint Checks

Fully load the tip of a no. 12 flat brush with Limeade PermEnamel. Brush checks around the border of the plate (see page 23).

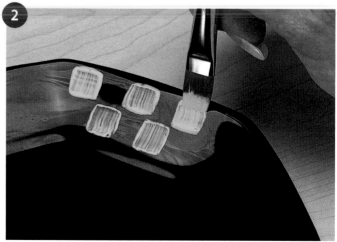

☆ Helpful Hint

When using PermEnamel paints, keep your brush out of water except when cleaning or changing color. Then, dry-wipe it. Delta PermEnamel paint does not mix well with water.

32

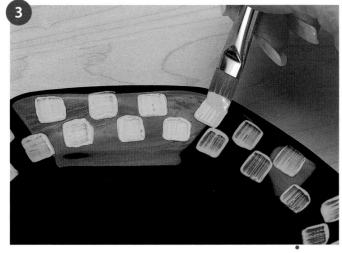

3

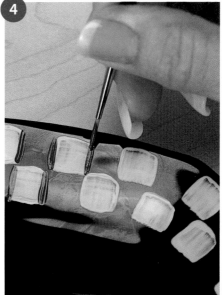

4

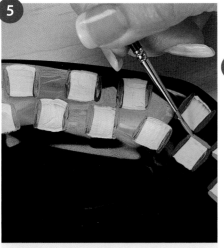

5

6

3. Add Second Coat

When the paint is dry, it no longer has a shiny cast to it. Add a second coat of paint to your checks.

4. Outline Sides

With a no. 1 Jackie Shaw liner brush, outline the sides of each check with Hunter Green.

5. Outline Tops and Bottoms

Load the same liner with True Green and outline the top and bottom of each check.

6. Paint Roses

Load a no. 3 round brush with Red Red and paint large dots inside the checked border with circular strokes. These will become the roses.

Helpful Hint

When working with PermEnamel paints, if the paint gets gooey, add a drop of Delta Thinner to your puddle to keep it liquid. It is great!

7. Paint Leaves

Load the same no. 3 round brush with True Green and make leaves on the sides of each rose. Begin with a single stroke for one side of the leaf. Make the stroke thick at the base, coming to a point at the end.

8. Complete Leaves

Paint the second stroke to complete each leaf.

9. Add More Red

Paint a second coat of Red Red on the roses.

10. Detail Leaves

With a no. 1 Jackie Shaw liner brush, pull a center vein for each leaf using Hunter Green. With the same liner brush, highlight the ends of the leaves with Limeade, pulling eight strokes into the leaves, four on each side.

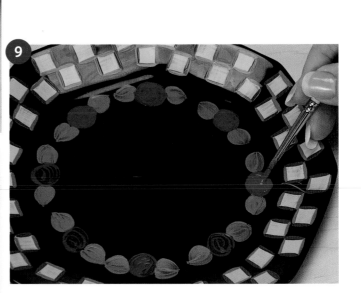

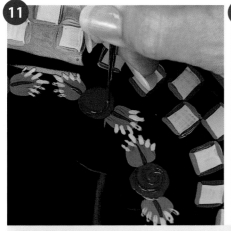

11.

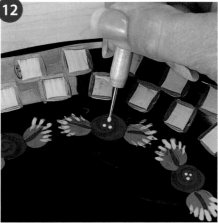

12.

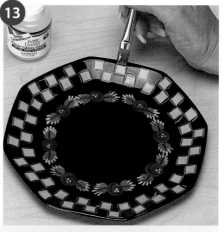

13.

11. Paint Spirals

Using the same liner brush, paint a spiral on the center of each rose with Light Burgundy. Start from the edge of the red dot and work into the center.

12. Dot Roses

Dip the tip of a stylus into Cotton Candy Pink to make the three little dots in the center of each rose.

13. Allow to Dry and Cure

Once all the paint is dry to the touch, apply a clear gloss glaze to the areas you have painted. Store your project in a safe place to dry and cure for ten days before use.

☆ Helpful Hint

When working on any piece that is glass or ceramic, I use a gloss glaze for shiny surfaces and a satin glaze for etched or frosted surfaces.

Mix Things Up!

I love working with PermEnamel paints because of the enormous variety of surfaces available to use them on. And preparing to paint on colored glass is so easy—
no sanding, dusting, sealing or basing a background color! Not only can you add a new and fun look to your dinner table, but you can also display your art as part of the kitchen or dining room décor. How cool is that? Remember to use other surface colors as well.

Plaid Floor cloth

I love plaids! My family
roots are Irish and Scottish, and we are
represented by two beautiful plaids for the Scotts
and the Camerons. Plaids have always been very popular in home décor and probably will never go out of style,
so why not develop plaids to paint on floor coverings and
furniture? For those of you who prefer straight, equal and
accurate, this motif is for you. If you like loose, wavy and uneven,
this motif could also be for you. For any plaids, the key is
repetition. So keep the same type of brushstrokes—
either straight or wavy—throughout
the design.

Materials

Gesso treated canvas floorcloth (enough for a ½ circle (18" × 36") [46cm × 92cm])

3" (76mm) foam craft roller

Sea sponge

Ruler

Tape

Pennies

Varnish

⅜-inch (10mm) rake brush

½-inch (12mm) rake brush

¾-inch (19mm) wash/glaze brush

No. 2 script liner brush

No. 12 flat brush

Delta Ceramcoat Paints

Old Parchment	Trail Tan	Green Sea	Antique Gold
Purple Dusk	Forest Green	Raw Sienna	Moroccan Red
White			

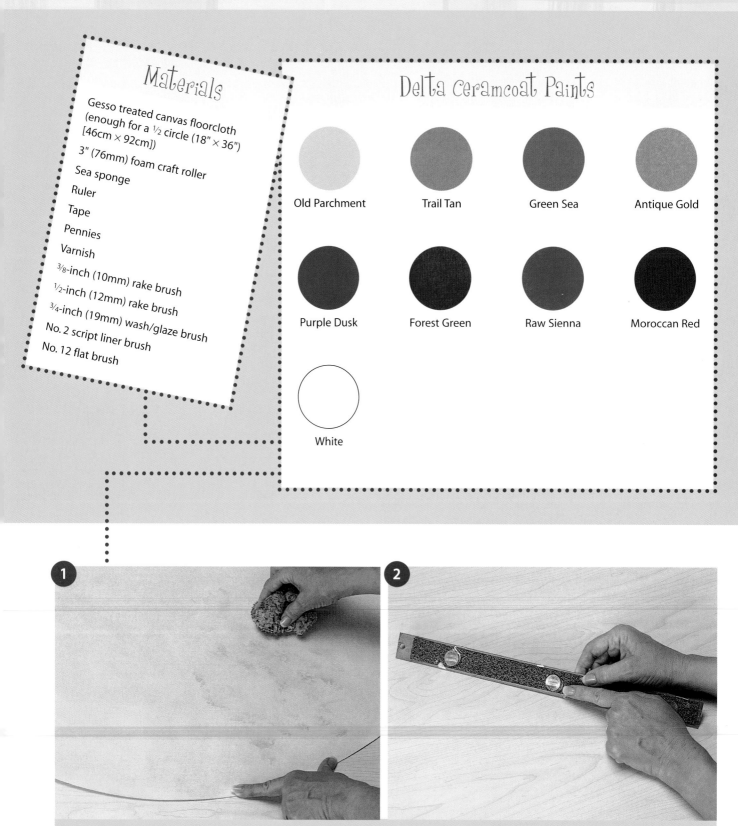

1. Basecoat Floor Cloth

Basecoat a floor cloth with Old Parchment using a 3" (76mm) foam craft roller. Allow this to dry well. When completely dry, sponge the surface with a sea sponge (see page 21) and a wash of Trail Tan. Keep the paint light.

2. Prepare Ruler

Tape even stacks of three pennies to the bottom of a ruler to elevate it from the surface. By doing this, you will keep the paint from sliding below the ruler.

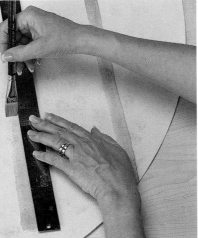

3. Paint Green Lines

Place the ruler on the floorcloth in a vertical direction and use this as a guide to make the lines.

Fully load a ¾-inch (19mm) wash brush with a wash of Green Sea paint and pull a vertical line up the floorcloth. Measure 5½" (14cm) from the edge of the first line and repeat. (For loading a wash brush, see page 16).

4. Paint Gold Lines

Fully load a no. 12 flat brush with a wash of Antique Gold and paint a second series of lines 2½"(6cm) to the left of the green lines.

5. Paint Purple Lines

Load a ½-inch (12mm) rake brush with a wash of Purple Dusk and paint a series of purple lines about 1½" (4cm) to the left of the green lines. At this point, you will no longer need the ruler as a guide; just paint between the lines you have already established. It is okay if your lines are not perfect. A little wiggle just adds character!

6. Paint Forest Green Lines

To the left side of each Green Sea line, use the ½-inch (12mm) rake brush to pull a line of Forest Green. To make the lines a bit narrower, simply angle the brush.

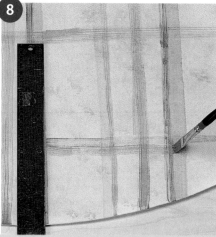

7. Paint Raw Sienna Lines

Load a ⅜-inch (10mm) rake brush with Raw Sienna and pull a line just on the right side of the gold lines.

8. Begin Horizontal Stripes

Load a ½-inch (12mm) rake brush with Raw Sienna and pull two horizontal stripes side by side to create a double-wide stripe on the floorcloth. Space the next double-wide stripe 5" (13cm) below the first and repeat. Use the ruler as a visual guide.

9. Paint Green Raked Stripes

Using the ½-inch (12mm) rake brush, add a double-wide raked stripe of Forest Green about 3" (8cm) below the Raw Sienna stripes.

10. Paint Purple Raked Stripes

Add single raked stripes of Purple Dusk, using the ⅜-inch (10mm) rake brush, just below the gold stripes.

11. Add More Vertical Lines

Load a script liner brush with Forest Green and pull vertical lines to the right of each wide Green Sea line. Load the same script liner with Moroccan Red and pull a line to the left of the vertical gold lines.

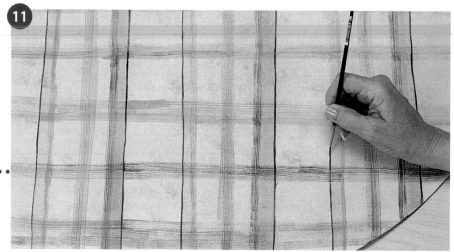

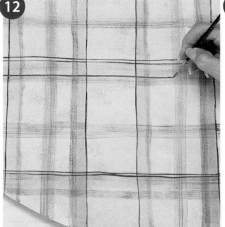

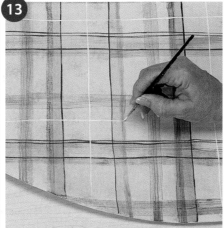

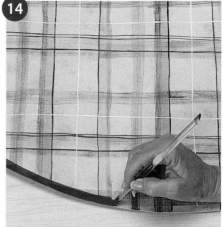

12. Add More Horizontal Lines

With the same script liner brush and Moroccan Red, add additional horizontal double lines above the raked Raw Sienna lines. Then add a single line of Purple Dusk between the horizontal lines of Raw Sienna and Purple Dusk.

13. Add White Lines

Load the script liner brush with white and paint vertical lines in the large gap between the Forest Green and the Moroccan Red lines. Next, paint horizontal lines in white between the double line of Moroccan Red and raked stripe of Forest Green.

14. Paint Border

Paint a one-coat border around the curved edge in Moroccan Red using the no. 12 flat brush. The flat edge of the floorcloth will be up against a door edge or a cupboard, therefore I did not paint the flat edge. Apply a few coats of varnish to your floorcloth to protect the finish. Be sure to allow one coat to dry thoroughly before adding another coat.

Mix Things Up!

As you paint more projects with this plaid motif, be sure to repeat the same pattern throughout. Try giving your project a green or purple border and see how this changes the entire look. For that matter, how about a red or green background and yellow border? I liked the cheerfulness of the background used here, but if you prefer one of the other palette colors, use it instead. You could even vary the original colors to match your own décor. The simpler the palette, the easier the project is to complete. Just have fun creating!

Floral & Weave
watering can

Do you wish your life
had a bouquet of happy and colorful
flowers in it? Well, now you can paint them on
anything you like to your heart's content. Here is an
easy ribbon-weave motif that makes a great border for
any surface. You can also paint some fun flowers to go on
your favorite watering can or flowerpot. Create a bouquet
full of blooms, or limit your piece to a single flower. No matter
what direction you choose, your love for this design is sure
to grow!

Materials

Galvanized watering can
Rubbing alcohol
Soft cloth
Tracing paper
Pencil
White graphite paper
Stylus
Varnish
No. 1 script liner brush
No. 1 Jackie Shaw liner brush
No. 4 round stroke brush
No. 6 filbert brush
No. 8 flat shader brush
No. 12 flat shader brush
3/8-inch (10mm) angular brush
3/4-inch (19mm) wash/glaze brush

Delta ceramcoat Paints

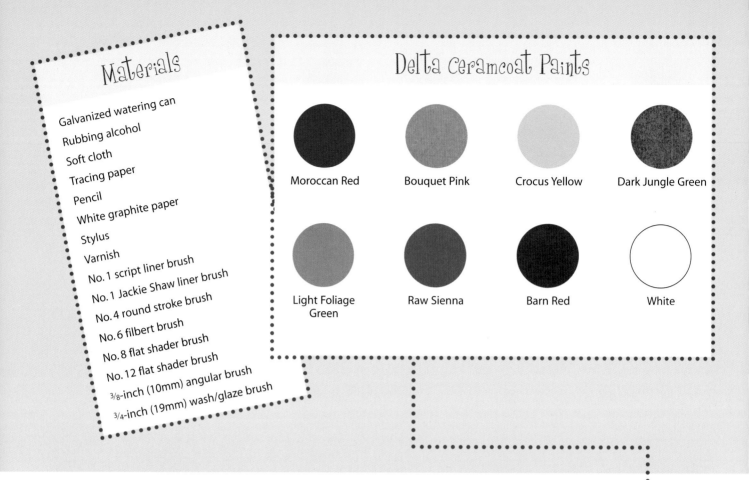

Moroccan Red Bouquet Pink Crocus Yellow Dark Jungle Green

Light Foliage Green Raw Sienna Barn Red White

1. Prepare Watering Can

Clean a galvanized watering can with alcohol (see page 13) and basecoat it with two coats of Moroccan Red using a ¾-inch (19mm) wash/glaze brush. After it is completely dry, apply the pattern lines using a stylus and white graphite paper placed between the surface and your traced pattern (see page 88 for pattern). With a no. 6 filbert brush, base-coat the six petal flowers in Bouquet Pink and the tulip petals in Crocus Yellow. Add a second coat if needed.

2. Basecoat Leaves and Stems

Basecoat the petal flower leaves and stems with Dark Jungle Green. Basecoat the tulip leaves and stems in Light Foliage Green.

3

4

5

6

3. Basecoat Flower and Border

Basecoat the center of the six petal flower with Raw Sienna. Fully load a no. 12 flat shader brush with Light Foliage Green and paint a large horizontal band of ribbon for the lower border.

4. Paint Vertical Bands and Handle

With a no. 8 flat shader brush, paint the vertical bands Crocus Yellow so that every other ribbon is over or under the green band. These yellow bands are approximately 1" (25mm) apart. Paint the handle of the watering can with a yellow band. Add a second coat if needed.

5. Shade Flowers

Shade floated color (see page 17) around the center of the petal flowers with Barn Red using a side-loaded 3/8-inch (10mm) angular brush. Use the same method to shade between the tulip petals with Raw Sienna. Side load the brush with Dark Jungle Green and paint the vein lines of the leaf and the stem.

6. Outline Leaves and Veins

Use the no. 1 Jackie Shaw liner brush (see page 18) to outline the leaves of the six petal flower in Light Foliage Green. Paint a swirl in the center of each leaf for a vein.

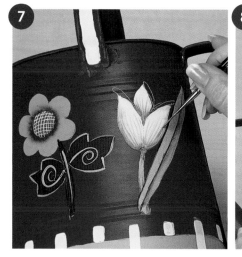

7. Paint Crosshatch Lines

Place crosshatch lines (equally spaced lines crossing over each other) in the center of the six petal flower with Crocus Yellow using the same liner brush. Add a few long lines to the tulip petals with Raw Sienna, starting at the base of the flower.

8. Outline Ribbon and Petals

Using White and the same liner, outline the yellow ribbons and the petals on the flower.

9. Paint Comma Strokes

Using the no. 4 round stroke brush and White, paint long comma strokes (see page 20) on the top of each tulip flower. Bring the right petal stroke to the bottom of the flower.

10. Add Green Lines

Add lines to the top and bottom of the green band with Dark Jungle Green using a script liner.

11. Add Wavy Line

Add a wavy line in Crocus Yellow along the center of the green ribbon band using a no. 1 script liner.

12. Add Red Dots

With the end of a medium-handled paint brush, add dots of Barn Red to the middle of the yellow ribbons on the border and the handle.

13. Add Yellow Dots

Use a stylus to add tiny dots of Crocus Yellow around the center of the six petal flowers. To protect your painted piece, brush with varnish, allowing the varnish to dry thoroughly between coats.

Mix Things Up!

So you want to use the hottest colors? This red watering can could not be hotter, but you could also use a yellow background. Check out the cute yellow flower pot, for example. Use some dimensional flowers painted with the same colors that appear on the pot. Or, just use the ribbon weave for a flower box, as shown. These are sure to brighten any patio décor. How about putting the ribbon weave on a serving tray? I'm sure you will come up with your own creative ideas for using these patterns and great warm colors. Have fun!

Cookies & Candy candle

Everyone loves candy
and cookies. Rest assured, these items
were designed with a low-fat and zero-sugar
recipe! But they are a blast to paint. Kids especially
love this project. Try painting some ornaments and let
the kids help you hang them. With this project, you'll learn
to "bake" your cookies and add sugar to your gumdrops
with a stippler. You'll also create your candies by floating
color with an angular brush. For a reminder on using these
brushes, refer to page 21 for using a stippler and
page 17 for floating color with a
side-loaded brush.

Materials

- Candle
- Rubbing alcohol
- Soft cloth
- Candle and soap medium
- Tracing paper
- Graphite paper
- Stylus
- Eraser-capped pencil
- No. 1 Jackie Shaw liner brush
- No. 5 round brush
- ¼-inch (6mm) stippling brush
- ½-inch (12mm) stippling brush
- ⅜-inch (10mm) angular brush
- ¾-inch (19mm) wash/glaze brush
- Water-based satin varnish

Delta Ceramcoat Paints

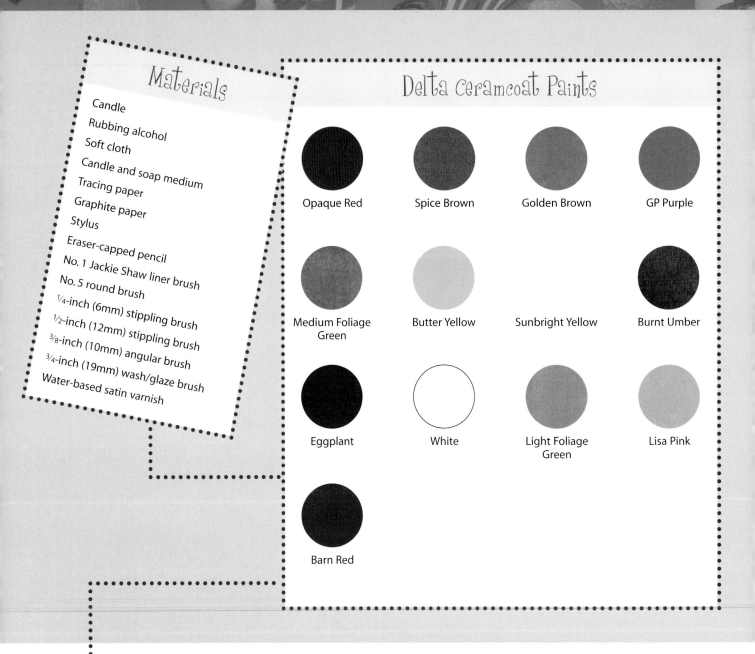

Opaque Red	Spice Brown	Golden Brown	GP Purple
Medium Foliage Green	Butter Yellow	Sunbright Yellow	Burnt Umber
Eggplant	White	Light Foliage Green	Lisa Pink
Barn Red			

1. Clean Candle

Clean the candle with rubbing alcohol on a soft cloth.

2. Apply Candle and Soap Medium

Using a ¾-inch (19mm) wash/glaze brush, apply the candle and soap medium to the candle. This will prepare the surface to hold the paint without it beading up.

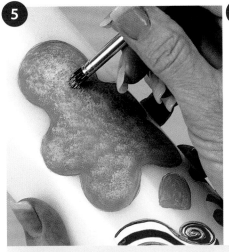

3. Basecoat Candies

Apply the basic outline pattern (see page 89 for pattern) with graphite paper, pressing lightly into the candle with a stylus. Using the no. 5 round brush, basecoat the candies with White, the chocolate chips with Spice Brown and the gingerbread cookie with Golden Brown.

4. Add Candy Details

Basecoat the gumdrops in GP Purple with the no. 5 round brush. Add the Medium Foliage Green stripes to the ribbon candy with a no. 1 Jackie Shaw liner. Paint Opaque Red stripes on the peppermint candy.

You can also basecoat the gumdrops with Light Foliage Green, Lisa Pink or Sunbright Yellow.

5. Stipple Gingerbread Cookie

Using Butter Yellow and a ½-inch (12mm) stippling brush, stipple the gingerbread cookie to ⅛" (3mm) from the edge. Next, stipple the center rounded areas with Sunbright Yellow to add highlights. Use a "dirty" brush (see page 21) to help blend the colors. Wipe off excess paint by rubbing your brush on a soft cloth. The brush will still have a bit of color in it. Apply the next color, continuing the stippling. As long as your paint colors are in the same color family (e.g., yellow/gold, red/pink), your stipple colors will blend nicely.

6. Shade Cookies

Side load a ⅜-inch (10mm) angular brush with Spice Brown and float around the outside of the cookie. In the same manner, float Burnt Umber on the chocolate chips to shade.

☆ Helpful Hint

When stippling, if you apply too much of one color, stipple the background color from the edge back into the design.

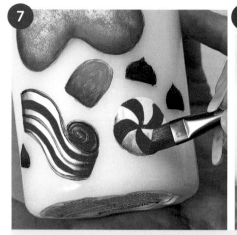

7. Shade Candies

Using the same ⅜-inch (10mm) brush, shade the purple gumdrop with a side load of Eggplant

In the same manner, shade the yellow gumdrops with Butter Yellow, the green with Medium Foliage Green and the pink with Opaque Red. Shade the peppermint and ribbon candies on the bottom side lightly with Barn Red.

8. Paint Gingerbread Icing

Use a no. 1 Jackie Shaw liner with White to paint a wavy icing border on the gingerbread cookie. Using the eraser, or flat end of a pencil, dab three White buttons down the center of the cookie. Allow these to dry well.

9. Add Eyes and Nose

With the no. 1 Jackie Shaw liner and Burnt Umber, paint the branch lines for the pine needles above the gingerbread. Place chocolate chip strokes (see page 19) for the eyes and nose.

10. Paint Cheeks

To make the gingerbread mouth, paint two dots of equal size on each cheek using a double-ended stylus and Opaque Red. Use this color to paint swirls on the peppermint candy buttons as well.

11. Add Smile

Using the no. 1 Jackie Shaw liner brush, connect the dots with a curved mouth line.

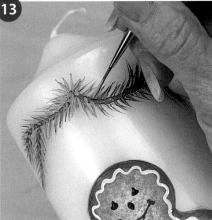

12. Add Highlights

With the same liner and White, paint the rounded comma stroke (see page 20) on the top side of each peppermint candy for a highlight.

13. Paint Pine Needles

Paint the pine needles with the liner and Medium Foliage Green. Then add fewer strokes of Light Foliage Green on top. These needles can be straight or slightly curved, long or short.

14. Stipple Gumdrops

Use a ¼-inch (6mm) stippling brush and White to stipple the tops of the gumdrops. Protect your gingerbread and candy candle by applying a brush-on satin varnish to the surface.

Mix Things Up!

Gingerbread and candies are always so popular around the holidays. What could be more wonderful than creating something to put a smile on someone's face? Go bake some cookies and decorate them to look like these. Can you imagine the delight of the recipient if you painted a plate and then added the "real thing" on top as a gift? Fabulous! Or paint a candy dish and fill it with the types of candies you painted. Glass dishes and plates can be found at your nearest discount department store. They are inexpensive, but what an impact you can make with this gift to yourself or someone else!

Kids' Bugs frame

Cute
and colorful bugs are
sure to put smiles on kids' faces. These
are done with a stroke technique, so when you
use the proper brush, you can basecoat each area of
these cute little critters (head, bodies, wings and so on)
with one easy stroke. As you'll see in this motif, sometimes
fewer strokes are better, but there is no end to the variety of
bugs you can create. You might even find yourself creating
a new species! Don't limit yourself to painting bugs on this
frame. Your kids will love having bugs on their
walls and furniture as well.

Materials

Frame
All-purpose sealer
Sandpaper
Double-ended stylus
Tracing paper
Pencil
Gray graphite paper
Varnish
No. 1 Jackie Shaw liner brush
No. 4 round stroke brush
No. 4 filbert brush
No. 6 filbert brush
No. 8 flat shader brush
¼-inch (6mm) deerfoot stippler

Delta PermEnamel Paints

White

Blue Danube

GP Purple

Pineapple Yellow

Lisa Pink

Antique Gold

Apple Green

Black

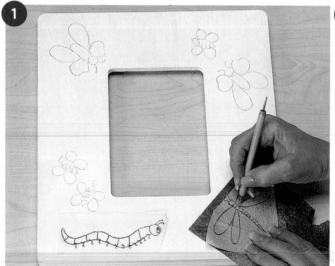

1. Prepare Frame

Seal the frame with a coat of sealer, then lightly sand. Basecoat the frame White. Transfer the bug pattern onto the frame using a double-ended stylus with gray graphite paper between the frame and pattern (see page 88 for pattern).

2. Basecoat Butterflies

With a no. 6 filbert brush, basecoat the butterfly bodies in GP Purple. Paint one round stroke for the head and two long strokes for the body. Basecoat the upper wings of one butterfly and the lower wings of the second with Pineapple Yellow. Start at the outer edge and bring the stroke toward the body.

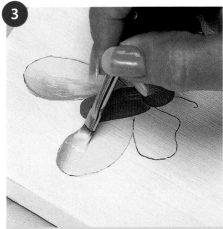

3. Shade Wings

Fully load the no. 6 filbert brush with Pineapple Yellow, then dip one corner into Lisa Pink to double load. Hold the pink side of the brush against the body and shade the yellow wings.

4. Basecoat Other Wings

Basecoat the other sets of wings with your choice of palette colors. I used Lisa Pink and Blue Danube.

5. Highlight Pink Wings

Load the no. 6 filbert brush with Lisa Pink and then dip it into Pineapple Yellow to float highlights along the bottoms of the wings.

6. Highlight Blue Wings

Float highlights on the blue wings with the same technique, loading the brush with Blue Danube and dipping it into Pineapple Yellow.

7. Shade Yellow Wings

Shade the yellow wings with the same technique, loading the brush with Pineapple Yellow and dipping it into Blue Danube.

8

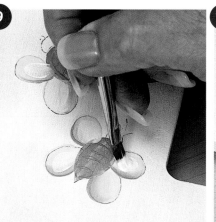

9

10

8. Basecoat Bees' Bodies

With a no. 4 filbert brush, basecoat the bee bodies with Antique Gold and the bee wings with Pineapple Yellow.

9. Add Highlights

Side load the no. 4 filbert brush with Antique Gold and float onto the lower edges of the wings. Clean the brush and place a stroke of White in the center of each wing for a highlight.

10. Paint Dragonfly Wings

Using the no. 6 filbert brush, basecoat the lower dragonfly wings in Lisa Pink and the upper wings in Pineapple Yellow. Dip the already yellow brush into GP Purple and float along the top side of the yellow wing.

11. Paint Tops of Pink Wings

Load the no. 6 filbert brush with Lisa Pink and dip into GP Purple. Float along the tops of the pink wings.

12. Basecoat Caterpillar

Basecoat the sections of the caterpillar with a no. 8 flat brush. Start with Apple Green for the head and alternate with your choice of the five colors.

11

12

13. Stipple Edges

Stipple the edges (top and bottom) with like colors using a ¼-inch (6mm) deerfoot stippler (see page 21).

14. Fill in Details

Using a no. 4 round stroke brush and Black, fill in the bee heads, dragonfly body and caterpillar eye.

15. Outline Bugs

With the no. 1 Jackie Shaw liner, outline all the bugs in Black. Include the antennae, stripes on the bees and feet and lines on the caterpillar.

When outlining these delightful bugs, it is not necessary to be exact or to complete the line. Sometimes just a hint of a line is best.

16. Trim Frame Edge

Trim the edge of the frame with the no. 8 flat shader brush and Apple Green—or any fun palette color of your choice. To protect your finished piece, brush with varnish and allow to dry thoroughly between coats.

Mix Things Up!

Can you just imagine a wall of these cute critters? This fun and fast design will give a great new lift to a child's room. Try painting them on a dresser, wastebasket, mirror frame, lampshade, bed or side table to give the room a fun and colorful change. Then just listen for the kids to giggle with delight.

Fall Leaves
table runner

The arrival of autumn is one of my favorite times of the year. The landscape reminds me of a painter's palette: so beautiful in colors of red, yellow, orange and green. I chose a motif of simple autumn leaves and acorns perfect for decorating a fall dining table. The rich colors carry over nicely to napkins and candles, as well. I've also provided a simple faux background technique that is great for walls and furniture. These colors put me in the mood for hot soup and cornbread!

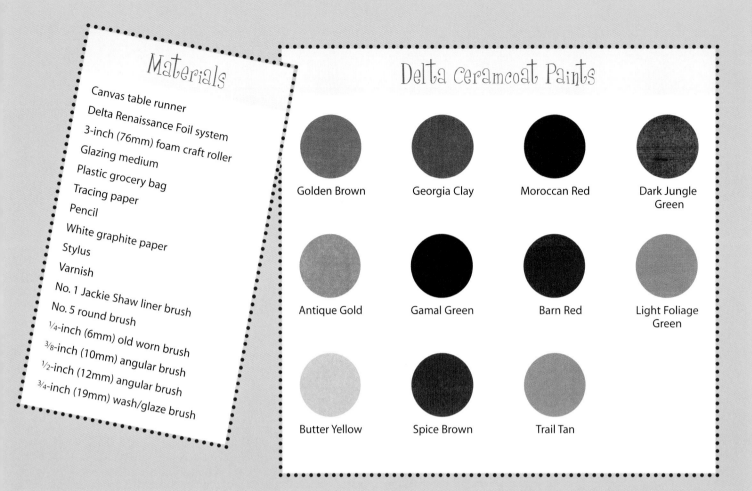

Materials

Canvas table runner

Delta Renaissance Foil system

3-inch (76mm) foam craft roller

Glazing medium

Plastic grocery bag

Tracing paper

Pencil

White graphite paper

Stylus

Varnish

No. 1 Jackie Shaw liner brush

No. 5 round brush

1/4-inch (6mm) old worn brush

3/8-inch (10mm) angular brush

1/2-inch (12mm) angular brush

3/4-inch (19mm) wash/glaze brush

Delta Ceramcoat Paints

Golden Brown	Georgia Clay	Moroccan Red	Dark Jungle Green
Antique Gold	Gamal Green	Barn Red	Light Foliage Green
Butter Yellow	Spice Brown	Trail Tan	

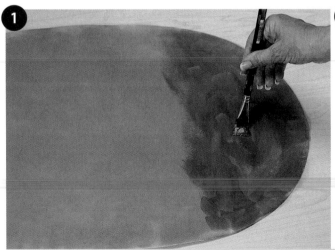

1. Prepare and Basecoat Canvas

See page 13 for directions on adhering the canvas to a backing to stabilize it for painting on. Using a 3-inch (76mm) foam craft roller, basecoat the canvas surface (see page 15) with Golden Brown. Once the paint is completely dry, mix a glaze of two parts glazing medium with one part Georgia Clay. Brush this glaze in workable-sized areas with a 3/4-inch (19mm) wash/glaze brush.

2. Texture Surface

Cover your hands with a plastic grocery bag and place the bag over the glazed area. Without moving the bag, just your hand, press down and then gently lift the bag. The more crumpled the bag, the more texture you will get. Brush on more glaze, overlapping when needed, and repeat the texturing process over the entire surface. Allow the surface to dry well.

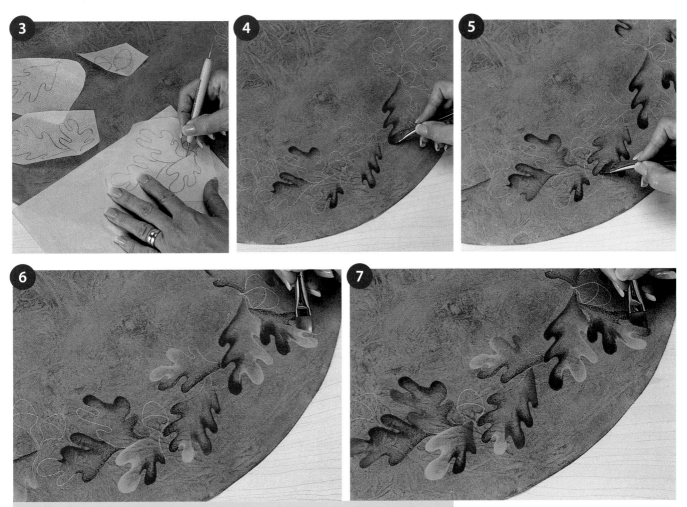

3. Transfer Pattern

Use white graphite paper and a stylus to trace on your leaf and acorn pattern (see page 90 for pattern) in an attractive grouping.

4. Shade Leaves

Begin painting the leaves with a ½-inch (12mm) angular brush. With Moroccan Red, make C-strokes (see page 19) to randomly shade some of the leaves.

5. Apply More Shading

Make the same random strokes on the leaves with Dark Jungle Green.

6. Blend Colors

Paint additional C-strokes with Antique Gold. Overlap the strokes of different colors slightly for a flawless blending and more natural-looking coloration.

7. Add Georgia Clay

Finally, add C-strokes of Georgia Clay, again overlapping the strokes to blend the colors.

Since these colors are all placed in random order, any leaf could have two, three or four colors. You decide.

Helpful Hint

When working with multiple colors, in a random fashion, work all over the surface using one color. Then, switch to the next color and repeat the process until you have used all the palette colors.

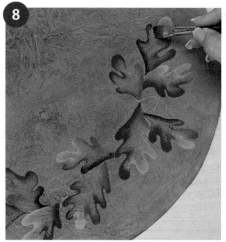

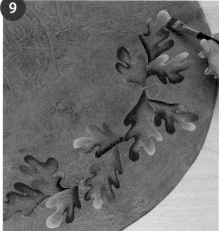

8. Deepen Colors

To deepen leaf colors, add small touches of darker colors toward the base of each leaf. Add Gamal Green to Dark Jungle Green areas. Add Barn Red to Moroccan Red areas. Do not cover all the red and green areas, just those at the leaf base.

9. Add Highlights

To highlight the leaf colors, add touches of lighter tones to the tips of the leaves. Add Light Foliage Green to Dark Jungle Green areas. Add Butter Yellow to Antique Gold areas.

10. Add Veins

Load a no. 1 Jackie Shaw liner brush with Gamal Green and pull vein lines on all leaves.

11. Basecoat Acorns

Basecoat the acorns with a no. 5 round brush. Use Spice Brown for the caps and Trail Tan for the bottoms.

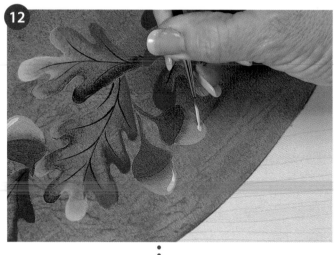

12. Add Comma Strokes

Side load a ³⁄₈-inch (10mm) angular brush and float Spice Brown just below the caps on top of the Trail Tan part of each acorn. Using a no. 1 Jackie Shaw liner brush and Butter Yellow, add a small comma stroke (see page 20) to the lower right side of each acorn.

13. Add Crosshatching

With the same liner and Antique Gold, add short highlight strokes to the acorn stems and crosshatching on the caps. Go back over the center of the crosshatching with Butter Yellow to brighten them.

14. Apply Adhesive to Border

With a ¼-inch (6mm) old worn brush, apply a glue border with foil adhesive. When the adhesive has lost its "milky" appearance and is dry, add a second coat and allow to dry until clear.

15. Place Foil Over Adhesive

With the dull side facing down, lay a foil piece over the glue and rub vigorously with your fingers. Remove the excess foil, place it on another section of adhesive and repeat. If you find you have missed an area of foil, reapply glue in that area, and allow it to dry before reapplying the foil sheet. When done, apply varnish to the entire piece, including the back of the canvas to take away any remaining stickiness from the spray adhesive.

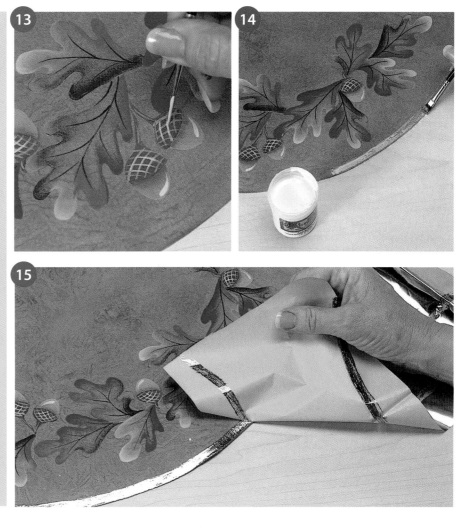

Mix Things Up!

Talk about a beautiful and fun table! These fall leaves and acorns are sure to please your family and guests. Also, consider painting this simple design on candlesticks and napkin holders. I bought some great papier mâché pumpkins to adorn the center of my table piece. They really worked well with the leaves and acorns to set the fall mood. Try wooden pumpkins, too! You can easily find green, orange and yellow candles and napkins to further embellish your beautiful design.

Butterfly lampshade

For you butterfly lovers,
this project will light you up every time
you look at it! I have painted the butterflies in
this project in primary colors (red, blue and yellow);
however, any color palette will work just as well. Butterflies are lovely in any color! Also, try using a colored ready-
made lampshade. When choosing a shade, it should be firm
on both the inside and the outside. Paint tends to bleed
through cloth shades unless you seal the underside first.

Lampshade

All-purpose sealer

Tracing paper

Pencil

Scissors

White graphite paper

Gray graphite paper

Double-ended stylus

Varnish

No. 1 Jackie Shaw liner brush

No. 6 filbert brush

3/8-inch (10mm) angular brush

1/2-inch (12mm) angular brush

1/2-inch (12mm) stippling brush

Delta ceramcoat Paints

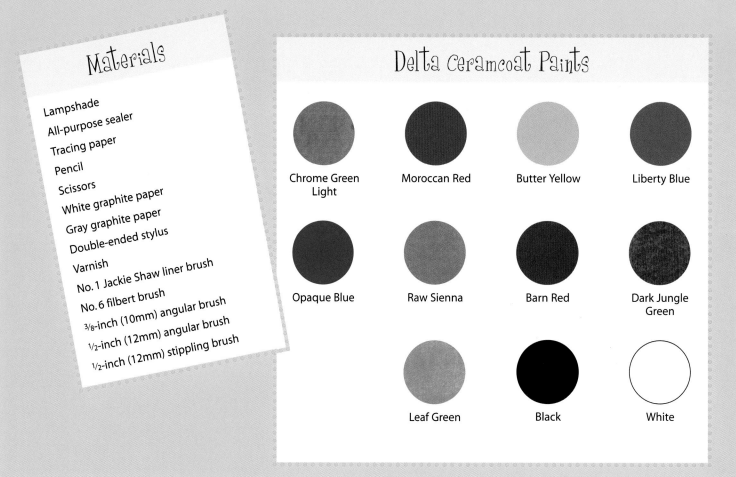

Chrome Green Light

Moroccan Red

Butter Yellow

Liberty Blue

Opaque Blue

Raw Sienna

Barn Red

Dark Jungle Green

Leaf Green

Black

White

1. Trace Shade Outline

Brush sealer on the inside of the lampshade to prevent the paint from bleeding through. When dry, roll the shade across a large sheet of tracing paper, marking the top and bottom. This will create a pattern of the correct size.

2. Copy Images

Cut the tracing paper out and copy the grass and butterfly images (see page 91) in a pleasing arrangement. Then, wrap the pattern around the shade and tape it in the back. Transfer the pattern with gray graphite paper, using a stylus. Trace only the outlines of the wings, not the details.

3. Basecoat Grass

With a no. 6 filbert brush, basecoat the grass with Chrome Green Light.

4. Basecoat Wings

Use the same brush to basecoat the wings of the butterflies. I used Moroccan Red, Butter Yellow and Liberty Blue. Leave a small gap between the wings to show where they overlap.

5. Add Details

Take the detailed pattern of the butterfly and transfer the details of the wings with graphite paper and a stylus. Use white graphite paper on the darker wings and gray graphite paper on the lighter wings.

6. Shade Butterflies

Using a ⅜-inch (10mm) angular brush, shade under the top wings on the lower wings. Shade the blue butterfly with Opaque Blue. Shade the yellow butterfly with Raw Sienna. Shade the red butterfly with Barn Red. When the wings are dry, use the same colors to float color along the wings next to the body.

7. Float Green Along Leaves

With the ½-inch (12mm) angular brush, float a shade of Dark Jungle Green along the leaves where they overlap each other and where the butterflies overlap them.

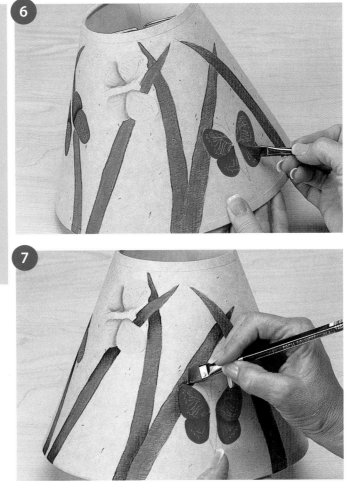

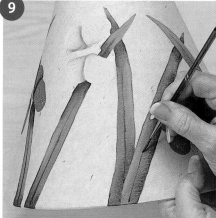

8. Highlight Leaves

With the same angular brush, highlight the leaves in Leaf Green, mostly toward the tip ends. Use the chisel edge of the brush and start at the point of the leaf.

9. Add Veins

Add leaf veins with the no. 1 Jackie Shaw liner brush in Dark Jungle Green.

10. Basecoat Bodies

Basecoat the bodies and outer edges of the wings in Black using the same liner brush.

11. Add Black Lines

Using your liner brush, place all the black lines on the wings.

12. Separate Body Segments

Side load the ³⁄₈-inch (10mm) angular brush with White and create the segments on the body.

13. Add Comma Strokes

Load the no. 1 Jackie Shaw liner brush with White and add all the white details with comma strokes (see page 20).

14. Add Dots

Using the large end of the double-ended stylus, add white dots near the body and on the wings. Slide the stylus a bit to make the elongated dots.

15. Apply Green Around Grass

With a ½-inch (12mm) stippling brush, apply some Chrome Green Light around the grass to complete the lampshade. To protect your lampshade, brush on a few coats of varnish. Allow to dry thoroughly between coats.

> ☆ **Helpful Hint**
>
> To further embellish any lampshade, add decorative fringe to the top and/or bottom of the shade.

Mix Things Up!

There are so many wonderful surfaces to use for this motif. Did you know that you can buy butterfly-shaped plates and wooden boxes to paint with this design? Also, how about painting a set of dishes with butterflies on them? You can use the Air-Dry PermEnamels, which are nontoxic and dishwasher safe, to change the look of your dining table. Scatter a few of these butterflies on a wall next to a dresser, or add them to your favorite picture frame. Whatever you do or wherever you place them, they are sure to be a show-stopper. Have fun with the colors, too!

Veggies canister

If you eat your veggies

every day, you know you'll grow up big
and strong. Well, if you don't like eating vegeta-
bles, maybe you'll love painting them in this soft,
muted but realistic style. Personally, I love to eat veggies
as much as I love to paint them. With this technique, the
colors can be made to look very washed and soft or bolder
with as much color as you like. This is a great motif to use in
the kitchen, but it also suits projects for the garden as well.
Harvest time is just around the corner!

Materials

Papier mâché canister

1½" (4cm) wooden knob

Glazing medium

Plastic grocery bag

Tracing paper

Gray graphite paper

Stylus

Coarse sponge

Pencil

Wood glue

Varnish

No. 1 Jackie Shaw liner brush

No. 6 filbert brush

No. 12 flat brush

½-inch (12mm) angular brush

¾-inch (19mm) wash/glaze brush

Delta Ceramcoat Paints

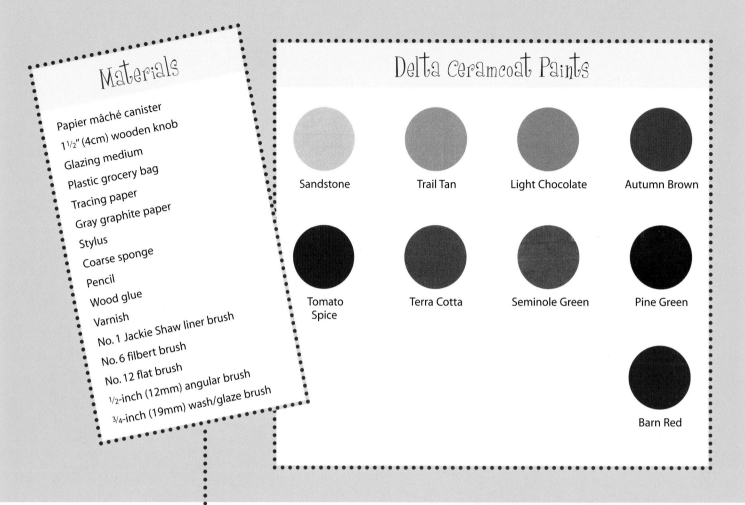

Sandstone

Trail Tan

Light Chocolate

Autumn Brown

Tomato Spice

Terra Cotta

Seminole Green

Pine Green

Barn Red

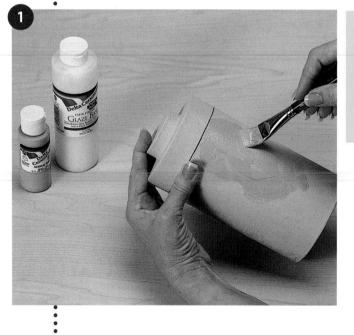

1. Prepare Canister

Basecoat the canister and wooden knob in Sandstone. Mix two parts glazing medium with one part Trail Tan. Using a ¾-inch (19mm) wash/glaze brush, quickly apply the mix on a workable area of the surface.

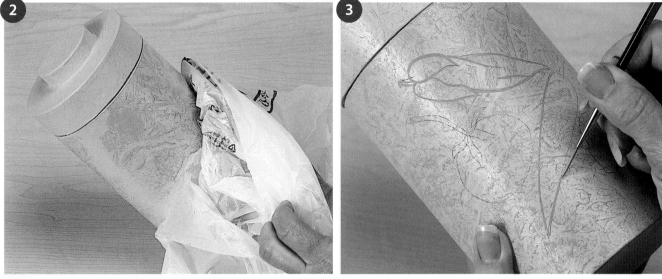

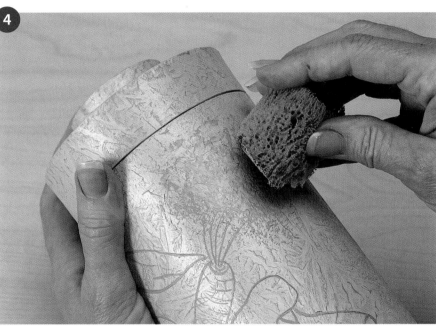

2. Texture Surface

Turn a plastic grocery bag inside out, and crumple it, then gently place the bag over the glazed area. Slide your hands around inside the bag, but do not move the bag itself. Remove the bag to reveal the crinkly texture. Repeat this process until the entire surface is textured. Allow to dry.

The more you crumple the bag, the finer the texture will be. If your glaze is too dark, pat it again with a clean section of bag to lift off more color.

3. Outline Veggies

When the glaze is dry, apply the veggie patterns (see page 92) with all details, using gray graphite paper and a stylus. Then, load the no. 1 Jackie Shaw liner brush with Light Chocolate and outline the veggies, including the detail lines. The knob on the lid will be painted as a tomato, though this is not in the pattern.

4. Sponge Carrot Top

Sponge the carrot top lightly with a small, coarse dampened sponge (see page 21) and Trail Tan.

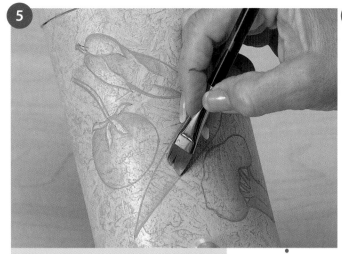

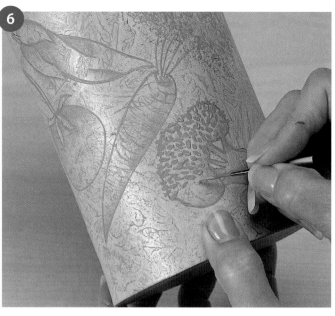

5. Float Shading on Veggies

Side load a ½-inch (12mm) angular brush with Light Chocolate and float it on the lower dark side of each veggie. Please refer to the picture to view where the dark areas are.

6. Make Sit-Down Strokes

Using the no. 1 liner brush and Light Chocolate, make "sit-down" strokes to color the broccoli florettes. This stroke is done by simply loading the end of the liner brush, placing it down on a surface and lifting it straight off. Continue this stroke in all directions

7. Shade Deep Areas

Use a touch of Autumn Brown and the ½-inch (12mm) angular brush to shade in the areas of the deepest shadows. This includes the portion of the carrot where the green lines are attached to the carrot top, or under the leaves of a tomato or chili. Shade the top of the tomato knob as well.

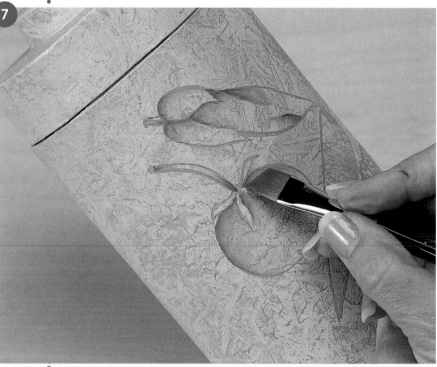

8. Wash Pepper and Tomatos

Using a no. 6 filbert brush, apply a wash of Tomato Spice to the red pepper and tomato. Use this wash to paint the wooden knob for the canister lid as well.

9. Wash Remaining Veggies

Apply a wash to the carrot with Terra Cotta, and a wash to the broccoli with Seminole Green. The leaves of the tomatos and the green pepper can be givin a wash with Pine Green. Then, pat the top of the broccoli with additional Pine Green for shading. Pat Barn Red on the tomatos and chili pepper to deepen the color on the shaded areas of each.

10. Color Stems and Greens

Use the no. 1 Jackie Shaw liner brush to paint the tops of the carrot stems in Pine Green. Sponge a watery wash of Seminole Green on the carrot greens. When this is dry, go over it with aditional sponging of Pine Green to shade the lower part of the carrot greens.

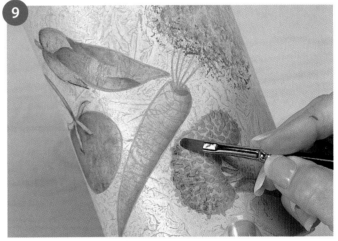

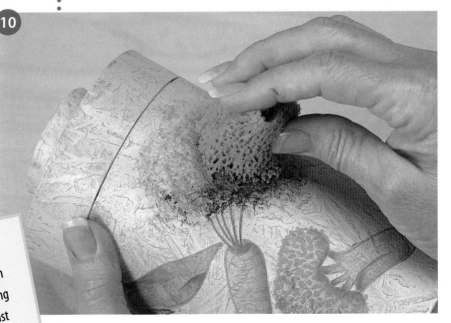

☆ Helpful Hint

To achieve a darker color for any image, it is best to add another wash of color over the first wash (repeating layers, if necessary), rather than just using a thicker layer of paint.

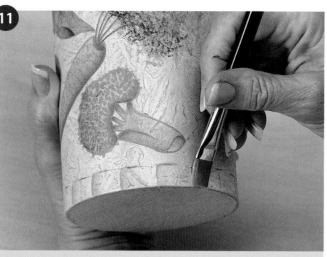

11. Make Checks

Draw pencil lines to mark the checks that are ½" × ½" (12mm × 12mm) along the lid and bottom of the canister. Shade the sides of each check using a no. 12 flat brush side loaded with Light Chocolate.

12. Color in Checks

Go over this float using a side-loaded bit of Autumn Brown.

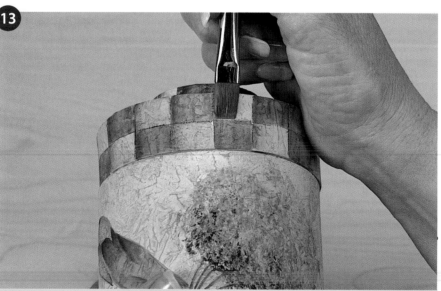

13. Add More Color

Color the checks with washes of Tomato Spice and Seminole Green using the same brush.

14. Outline Check Borders

Outline the borders of the checks with full-strength Tomato Spice on the liner brush.

15. Attach Knob

Place the wooden knob, which was painted as a cherry tomato in steps 8, 9 and 10, in the center of the canister lid and adhere with wood glue. Protect your canister by applying varnish to the finished piece. Be sure one coat is dry before applying another coat.

Mix Things Up!

I guarantee you'll get an abundance of compliments with this motif. It is an effective painting technique for "soft" and "bold" painters. You choose the degree of color you want. And don't stop with just the smaller projects. How about enlarging the veggie patterns and painting them on your walls, over the hood of your stove, on a kitchen cabinet or a tabletop? If the surface will be used frequently, be sure to apply several coats of varnish or a polyurethane finish to protect your work.

Lemons
table

If life deals you lemons,

paint a lemon table! Or, consider a lampshade, a bowl, a wastebasket or a picture frame.
These colorful lemons are bright, cheery and very
easy to paint. I instinctively love color, and yellow lemons
are one of my favorites. Wouldn't they be wonderful in the
middle of a plate or bowl? Or, how about a theme in a kitchen
on some cabinet doors? You can buy painted tiles and bowls
with lemons already painted on them, but now you can
very easily do it yourself!

Materials

20" (50cm) black metal table

Tracing paper

Scissors

Pencil

White graphite paper

Stylus

Seam ruler

White chalk pencil

Varnish

No. 1 Jackie Shaw liner brush

No. 4 filbert brush

No. 5 round brush

No. 12 angular brush

½-inch (12mm) angular brush

No. 12 flat brush

¼-inch (6mm) deerfoot stippler

½-inch (12mm) deerfoot stippler

No. 1 wash/glaze brush

Delta Ceramcoat Paints

 Sandstone

 Antique Gold

Seminole Green

 Raw Sienna

Butter Yellow

Bright Yellow

Pale Yellow

Gamal Green

 Leaf Green

White

1. Transfer Lemon Pattern

Cut a sheet of tracing paper to the size of your tabletop. Trace the pattern (found on page 93) on the tracing paper, arranging the design to fit. Alternate two lemons with one lemon and leaf. Place the tracing on the table and transfer the pattern onto the table with white graphite paper and a stylus.

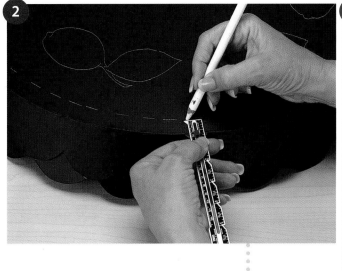

2. Mark Dotted Line

Use a seam ruler to measure ⅝" (16mm) from the edge of the table. Mark a dotted line as your guide with a white chalk pencil.

3. Basecoat Lemons and Stripes

Fully load a no. 5 round brush with Sandstone and basecoat the lemons, leaves and stems. Switch to a no.12 flat brush to basecoat stripes down the centers and ends of each scallop. Extend each stripe onto the tabletop, ending at the dotted line. Add three Sandstone checks on the lower scalloped sections.

4. Basecoat Checks and Lemons

Using Antique Gold, basecoat the lemons with the no. 5 round brush and then basecoat the checks with the no. 12 flat brush.

☆ Helpful Hint

A seam ruler is used in sewing and has a little red gauge on it that slides to mark your point of measure.

5. Shade Checks and Lemons

Basecoat the leaves with Seminole Green, using a no. 5 round brush. Side load a ½-inch (12mm) angular brush with Raw Sienna and shade the left side of each check and bottom third of each lemon.

6. Begin Stippling Lemons

Lightly load a ½-inch (12mm) deer-foot stippler brush with Raw Sienna and stipple the lower third of each lemon. Dry wipe the brush on a cloth and reload lightly with Butter Yellow. Starting at the top of the lemon, work this color down and very lightly over the top of the Raw Sienna.

7. Stipple Highlights

Continue stippling in the same manner with Bright Yellow and Pale Yellow, using fewer strokes with each lighter color to create the highlight in the upper center of the lemon. Work the stippling over each continuous color to blend the colors evenly, being careful not leave any lines of color.

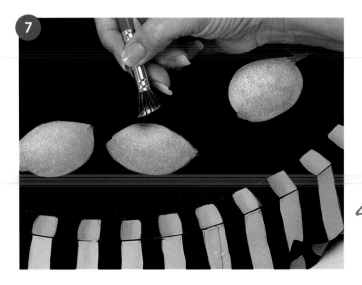

Helpful Hint

When stippling, if you stipple beyond the outer edge of the shape you are shading, wipe off the excess with a cotton swab. If it is already dry, you can paint a bit of the background color over it.

8. Add Veins

Use a no. 1 Jackie Shaw liner brush and Gamal Green to define the veins on the leaves. Add a wavy line to the center of the Sandstone stripes on the side of the table with the same color that is on the liner.

9. Float Green on Veins

Side load a no. 12 angular brush with Gamal Green and float this color below each vein line on the leaves.

10. Highlight Leaves and Lemons

With a ¼-inch (6mm) deerfoot stippler and a small amount of White, highlight the center of the highlight area of the lemon. Side load the ½-inch (12mm) angular brush with Leaf Green to highlight the leaves, floating color from the edges toward the center veins on the top side of the vein lines.

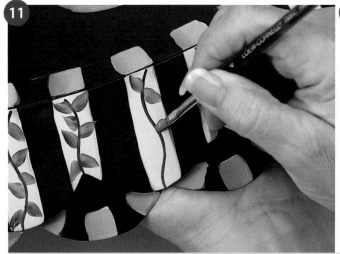

11. Paint Leaves

Double load a no. 4 filbert brush (see page 17) with Seminole Green and Gamal Green. To paint the border leaves, place the brush on the wavy line of the Sandstone stripe, pull slightly and twist and lift to a point. Change the direction of each leaf for variety and interest.

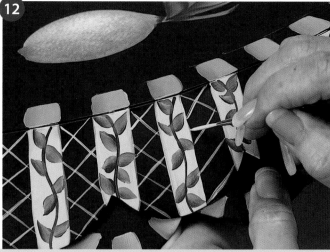

12. Add Crosshatching

On the remaining stripes, add crosshatching (equally spaced lines) with a no. 1 Jackie Shaw liner brush and Butter Yellow. I painted three to four lines in one direction and then crossed over with three to four lines in the opposite direction.

13. Add Line Border

Use the same liner brush to paint a line border along the stripes and around the checks with Seminole Green. This gives a nice clean look to all the stripes and checks.

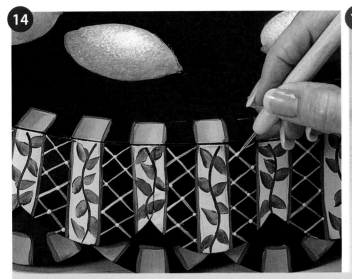

14. Add Dots

Finally, with a stylus and Butter Yellow, add dots at the inter-sections of the yellow lines. Be careful to stay out of these dots until they are dry! To keep the dots the same size, dip the stylus in the paint after each dot.

15. Varnish Table

Once all the paint is dry, use a no.1 wash/glaze brush to seal the table with several coats of varnish. Allow each coat to dry well before adding another coat.

Mix Things Up!

You'd be surprised at the "wows" you'll get with this project! Not only is it colorful, but it can be painted on so many wonderful surfaces. Try it on a series of place mats, for example. Remember that this design can be painted on other colored backgrounds as well; don't limit yourself to a black surface. I really liked the contrast of the black, but it would also look great on a lighter background. These tables are also available in an off-white color and a smaller size. (Please refer to the Resources list on page 94 for where to purchase them.) Don't you just love the scallops? Metal is so popular now, and it can be used anywhere in your home. What a great surface— useful, fun and creative!

Patterns

Enlarge this pattern 111% to bring to full size.

Floral & Weave Pattern (Page 42)

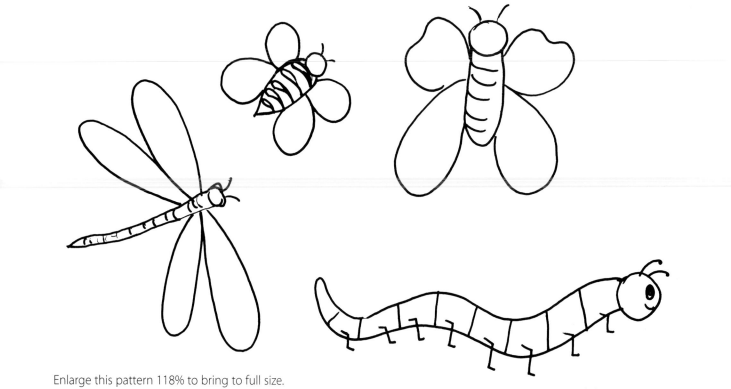

Enlarge this pattern 118% to bring to full size.

Kids' Bugs Pattern (Page 54)

This pattern is full size.

Cookies & Candy (Page 48)

This pattern is full size.

Fall Leaves Pattern (Page 60)

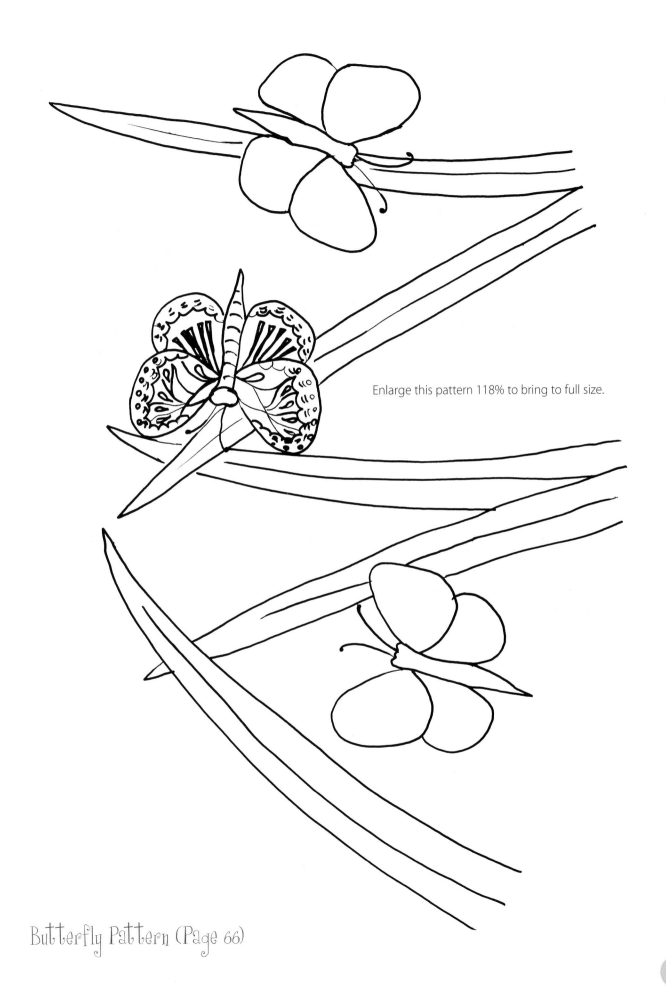

Enlarge this pattern 118% to bring to full size.

Butterfly Pattern (Page 66)

This pattern is full size.

Veggies Pattern (Page 72)

Enlarge this pattern 143% to bring to full size.

Solid line indicates
the edge of the table.

Lemons Pattern (Page 80)

Resources

Most of the materials used in this book can be found at your local arts and crafts store; and the surfaces can be found there, or at your local home store or discount department store. If you are unable to find any of the materials or surfaces, contact the manufacturers below for more information.

Retailers and Manufacturers in the United States

DCC (Decorator & Craft Corp)
428 S. Zelta St.
Wichita, KS 67207-1499
(800) 835-3013
Fax: (316) 685-7606
www.dcccrafts.com
(papier mâché, metal furniture)

Delta Technical Coatings, Inc.
2550 Pellissier Place
Whittier, CA 90601
(800) 423-4135
Fax: (562) 695-5157
www.deltacrafts.com
(acrylic and enamel paints and mediums)

Loew-Cornell, Inc.
563 Chestnut Ave.
Teaneck, NJ 07666
(201) 836-7070
Fax: (201) 836-8110
www.loew-cornell.com
(paint brushes and styluses)

Viking Woodcrafts, Inc.
1317 Eighth St. SE
Waseca, MN 56093
(800) 328-0116
Fax: (507) 835-3895
www.vikingwoodcrafts.com
(napkin rings, floorcloth and cut-outs)

Walnut Hollow Farm, Inc.
1409 State Road 23
Dodgeville, WI 53533-2112
(800) 950-5101
Fax: (608) 935-3029
www.walnuthollow.com
(platters, planter boxes, candle holders, frames and plates)

Retailers and Manufacturers in Canada

ChromaColour International
1410-28 Street NE
Calgary, Alberta T2A 7W6
www.chromacolour.com

Folk Art Enterprises, Inc.
P.O. Box 1088
Ridgetown, Ontario N0P 2C0
(800) 265-9434
www.folkartenterprises.com

MacPherson Craft Supplies
91 Queen St. E.
P.O. Box 1810
St. Mary's, Ontario N4X 1C2
(800) 238-6663
Fax: (519) 284-0858
www.macphersoncrafts.com

Maureen McNaughton Enterprises
RR #2
Belwood, Ontario N0B 1J0
(519) 843-5648

Mercury Art & Craft Supershop
332 Wellington Road
London, Ontario N6C 4P7
(519) 434-1636

Town & Country Folk Art Supplies
93 Green Lane
Thornhill, Ontario L3T 6K6
(905) 882-0199

Retailers in the United Kingdom

Art Express
Design House
Sizers Court
Yeadon LS19 6DP
0113 250 0077
Fax: 0113 250 0088
www.artexpress.co.uk

Green & Stone of Chelsea
259 Kings Road
London SW3 5EL
020 7352 0837
Fax: 020 7351 1098
www.greenandstone.com

Homecrafts Direct
P.O. Box 38
Leicester LE1 9BU
0116 269 7733
www.homecrafts.co.uk

Index

The best in decorative painting instruction and inspiration is from North Light Books!

Crafts from the Heart

Create thoughtful gifts for special friends and relatives using easy brush lettering and basic decorative painting strokes. Jan Belliveau has designed 8 lovely projects, each featuring an uplifting saying including a jewelry box, frame, tin wall sconce, tea caddy and more. You'll create exquisite gifts as you learn how to form your own brush letters, add flourishes and flowers, and develop your own unique style. ISBN 1-58180-464-4, paperback, 48 pages, #32721-K

Decorative Furniture with Donna Dewberry

Donna Dewberry shows you how to master her legendary one-stroke technique for painting realistic flowers, fruits and other decorative motifs. Simple step-by-step instructions accompany each project. Guidelines for matching color combinations to existing room schemes enable you to customize every project to fit your décor! ISBN 1-58180-016-9, paperback, 128 pages, #31662-K

Easy Christmas Projects You Can Paint

Create classic holiday decorations that everyone will love! You'll find 14 simple painting projects inside, from Santa figures and Christmas card holders to tree ornaments and candy dishes. Each one includes easy-to-follow instructions, step-by-step photographs and simple designs that you can use on candles, fabric or glass. ISBN 1-58180-237-4, paperback, 112 pages, #32012-K

Beautiful Brushstrokes

With Maureen McNaughton as your coach, you can learn to paint an amazing array of fabulous leaves and flowers with skill and precision. She provides start-to-finish instruction with hundreds of detailed photos. Beautiful Brushstrokes is packed with a variety of techniques, from the most basic stroke to more challenging, as well as 5 gorgeous strokework projects. ISBN 1-58180-381-8, paperback, 128 pages, #32396-K

These and other fine North Light titles are available from your local art & craft retailer, bookstore, online supplier, or by calling 1-800-448-0915